DATE DUE		
AUG 2 9 1990			
2 1			
FEB 1 0 1992			
OCT - 6 1992			
FEB 1 0 1993			
JAN 27 '94			
JUL 29 '96			
JAN 1 8 9			

DISTANCE
FLIGHTS

DISTANCE
FLIGHTS

DON BERLINER

Lerner Publications Company
Minneapolis

Maps of the distance flights can be found on pages 11, 14, 28, 50-51, 66-67.
Page 1: Three of the Douglas World Cruisers can be seen through the wing struts of the fourth.
Page 2: Louis Bleriot flies over the chalk cliffs of Dover, England, as he becomes the first to cross the English Channel in an airplane.

Library of Congress Cataloging-in-Publication Data

Berliner, Don.
Distance flights / Don Berliner.
p.   cm.
Includes index.
Summary: Describes great distance flights from the first successful crossing
of the English Channel by Louis Bleriot in 1909 to the circling of the earth
without refueling by Dick Rutan and Jeana Yeager in 1986.
ISBN 0-8225-1589-X (lib. bdg.)
1. Aeronautics—Flights—Juvenile literature.   2. Endurance flights—
Juvenile literature.   [1. Aeronautics—Flights.   2. Endurance flights.]   I. Title.
TL515.B424   1990
629.13'09—dc19
                                                                89-31261
                                                                CIP
                                                                AC

Manufactured in the United States of America

1 2 3 4 5 6 7 8 9 10 99 98 97 96 95 94 93 92 91 90

CONTENTS

Alex Henshaw flew from London, England, to Cape Town, South Africa, and back in his Percival Mew Gull, *pictured here.*

INTRODUCTION

During the early 20th century, travel became easier than ever before. Automobiles rolled onto city streets. Airplanes appeared in the skies.

Even though the automobile was safe, drivers still had to use roads and bridges to get where they needed to go. Pilots, on the other hand, could fly straight to their destinations. But in the early years, air travel wasn't entirely easy. Many flights ended abruptly with forced landings—and even crashes—in farmers' fields and remote countryside.

But soon, people were building airplanes that were flying farther and faster than ever before. It didn't matter what was down below. Pilots could fly across lakes and rivers, cruise over mountain ranges, and cross entire continents by air.

As aviation made its mark, people began to wonder. Was it possible to cross the treacherous English Channel in an airplane? What about the Atlantic Ocean? Could anyone actually fly *around the world* in one of these machines? Soon the race was on. Pilots wanted their names in the record books. They wanted to be the first and the fastest, but most of all—they wanted to fly farther than anyone had ever flown before.

Spectators watch Louis Bleriot in the early morning of July 25, 1909, as he heads out over the English Channel from the dunes near Calais, France.

Chapter 1

ACROSS THE ENGLISH CHANNEL

At its narrowest, the English Channel, the body of water that separates England and France, is 21 miles (34 kilometers) from shore to shore. Even so, it can be rough and dangerous to cross because of gusty winds, fog, or rain. Ever since the Normans invaded England 900 years ago, the Channel had kept England safe from foreign armies. The idea of an airplane crossing the Channel was both incomprehensible and exciting.

Early in 1909, an English newspaper offered a £1,000 prize to the first person to fly across the Channel. By summer, several pilots were camped outside of Calais, France. They were in the race to make the crossing.

The first pilot to try to fly across the Channel was Hubert Latham, a French playboy of English ancestry. On the morning of July 19, 1909, Latham took off. When he was less than halfway across the Channel, his engine stopped and his Antoinette *monoplane*, or single-winged plane, plopped into the water. Latham leaned back in his pilot's seat and lit a cigarette while he waited for the rescue boat.

A few miles from Latham's camp, another Frenchman, Louis Bleriot, set

up his camp and waited for the right weather. Bleriot had sent a French journalist, Charles Fontaine, across the Channel to search for the best spot for Bleriot to land.

At midnight on July 24, 1909, the wind started to slacken, and by 2:00 A.M. on July 25, the air was calm. Bleriot drove his plane out to the field overlooking the water. After a test flight before sunrise, he took off and headed west for England at 4:40 A.M. Among the people who saw Bleriot take off were friends of Latham. They wanted to make sure that Bleriot did not get a head start. They assumed this flight was just another test, but when Bleriot pointed the nose of his *Bleriot XI* monoplane out to sea, they knew he was on his way. By the time Latham had rushed out to the field, the wind was too strong; all he could do was stand and wait.

Bleriot's little airplane was one of the best of its day, but it was very crude by modern standards. It had no instruments to tell him how high he was or how fast he was flying, and it had no compass to direct him toward England.

Bleriot chugged along while a wind of more than 35 miles per hour (56 kilometers per hour) hit him in the face, as he had no windshield. As the morning got brighter, Bleriot could begin to make out the white chalk cliffs of Dover, England, in the distance. Soon he was

Journalist Charles Fontaine waves the French flag to signal where Bleriot should land.

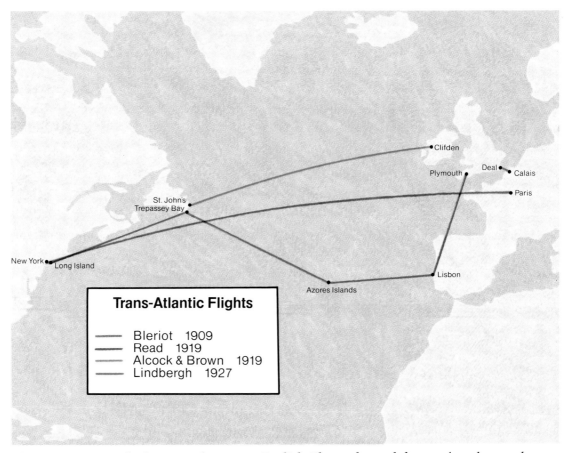

Bleriot's couragous flight across the stormy English Channel paved the way for others to dream about flying across the Atlantic Ocean. Before 20 years had passed, the Atlantic would be crossed non-stop and solo by Charles Lindbergh.

close enough to see people at the top of the cliffs, waiting for him.

Then he spotted Fontaine waving a French flag. Bleriot was over land and down for a hard landing near Deal. He had flown across the English Channel in 37 minutes.

Louis Bleriot averaged barely 35 mph (56 km/h). But he surprised the world with the first long over-water flight, as well as the first flight from one country to another. No longer could the stormy waters between England and France stop invading armies as they had done for centuries. The air was open to anyone who had the courage to use it.

Above: With spectators waving, Cal Rodgers takes off from a field on his way across the United States. Left: The Vin Fiz crashes nose-down in a field.

Chapter 2

ACROSS THE UNITED STATES

One of the first long-distance goals of airplane pilots was to fly all the way across the United States. In 1911, it was a long journey to travel from the Atlantic coast to the Pacific coast. Trains were slow, dirty, and uncomfortable. Over large parts of the country there were few decent roads on which cars could travel. If airplanes could make the cross-country trip, the two coasts would be brought closer together. Passengers, mail, and other cargo could travel quickly and easily from one coast to the other and back.

Newspaper publisher William Randolph Hearst put up a $50,000 prize for the first pilot to fly from coast to coast within 30 days. A month seems like a long time for a plane to take to cross the United States, but in 1911 airplanes flew so slowly and broke down so often that it was not long at all.

The third man to try for the prize was the tall, robust, nearly deaf Calbraith Perry Rodgers. He was a motorcycle racer who had soloed in an airplane after only 90 minutes of instruction. A few months after his first solo, he won $11,285 from the Aero Club of Illinois for flying 27 hours during a nine-day meet, an endurance record at the time.

The Wright brothers designed and built a *biplane*, or double-winged plane, especially for Rodgers's coast-to-coast flight. It was called the *Vin Fiz* after the grape-flavored soft drink made by the company that sponsored Rodgers's flight. Rodgers started off from New York on September 17, 1911, a month after he had won the Aero Club prize.

Rodgers flew during the daytime because he had no lights. He was accompanied by a special train carrying spare parts, mechanics, and his wife and mother. Rodgers had to fly around the highest mountains, since the *Vin Fiz*

could not climb over them. This made the trip longer. His 35-horsepower (26-kilowatt) engine could run for about 3½ hours on its 15 gallons (57 liters) of gasoline. At best, that would take him about 150 miles (241 km) before he had to stop to refuel.

On the first day, Rodgers flew from New York City to Middletown, New York—only 75 miles (121 km) away. The next day, September 18, he took off right into a tree and did so much damage to his airplane that it took three days for it to be repaired. His flight continued in much the same way: take off and

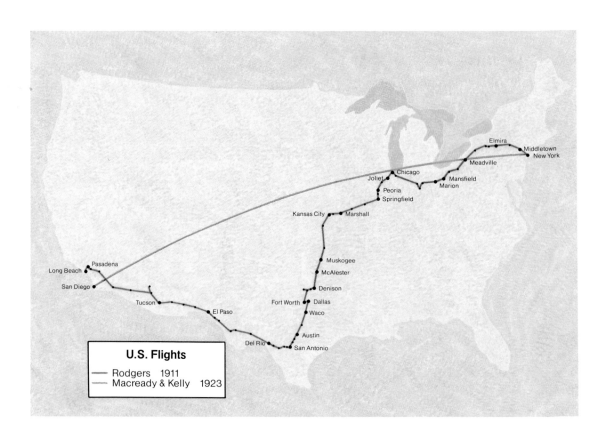

U.S. Flights
— Rodgers 1911
— Macready & Kelly 1923

crash, or fly for a while and crash, or glide down for a landing and crash.

Rodgers did not know much about navigating; he did not even have a compass to keep him pointed west. His simple plan to follow railroad tracks even got him into trouble. More than once he followed the wrong tracks away from a crossing and found himself far off course.

On the day that the time limit for Hearst's $50,000 prize ran out, Cal Rodgers flew from Springfield, Illinois to Marshall, Missouri. There was no way he could collect any money. But the attention and encouragement that he was getting from the newspapers and the public kept him going. Finally, after hopping across the country for 49 days,

he arrived in Pasadena, California. He had made nearly 70 stops and dozens of crash landings. The *Vin Fiz* had been repaired and rebuilt so many times that all he had left of the original airplane were two wing struts and the rudder.

Cal Rodgers's flight from New York to California took 82 hours of flying at an average of 52 mph (84 km/h). Since the 1950s, a cross-country trip on a commercial airliner has taken four or five hours. No one would dream of spending seven weeks hopping from field to field to make a trip that takes less than a week in a car on interstate highways. But in 1911, flying across the United States in 49 days made Cal Rodgers a celebrity and a hero.

Rodgers (left) stands beside the Vin Fiz *after completing his cross-country flight.*

The NC-4 lands on the Tagus River outside of Lisbon, Portugal, after successfully flying across the Atlantic Ocean.

Chapter 3

ACROSS THE ATLANTIC OCEAN

One of the greatest goals of the early long-distance flyers was to cross the Atlantic Ocean. They wanted to show that the airplane could connect Europe and North America more quickly and easily than could a ship. And so, as soon as airplanes were capable of making the long journey, pilots began to try.

In 1913, Lord Northcliffe, a British newspaper publisher, offered a prize equivalent to $50,000 for the first non-stop transatlantic flight. World War I intervened, and the first chance anyone had to fly across the Atlantic Ocean was delayed until 1919.

The U.S. Navy had built flying boats, or seaplanes, and decided to use them to cross the Atlantic on a navigational maneuver. The flying boats were not in competition for Lord Northcliffe's prize, as they would be stopping in Newfoundland, the Azores, and Portugal on their way from the United States to England.

Each Navy/Curtiss flying boat had four 400-horsepower (298-kw) V-12 engines, and its biplane wings stretched 126 feet (38 meters). When it was loaded with 1,600 gallons (6,060 l) of gasoline, it weighed 14 tons (13 metric tons). The NC could only fly 77 mph (124 km/h).

Floating on the Tagus River, the crew of the NC-4 *and other Navy officers look over the* NC-4 *before taking off for Plymouth, England.*

Led by Commander John Towers in the *NC-3*, all three flying boats—the *NC-1*, *NC-3*, and *NC-4*—took off on May 8, 1919, from Long Island, New York. They flew toward eastern Canada, but the *NC-4* was forced down at sea. It taxied on the water to Chatham, Massachusetts, was repaired, and flew on to meet the other two planes. On May 15, the three NCs finally reached Trepassey Bay, Newfoundland, the jumping-off point for the most dangerous part of the flight: 1,380 miles (2,220 km) over open water to the Azores.

The NCs had little navigation equipment for the long flight. To guide them, the U.S. Navy stationed 41 ships along their course. The ships would fire flares and point their searchlights to aid the NCs on the night portion of their flight.

For most of the flight, the NCs flew 1,000 feet (305 m) above sea level. But the three flying boats had to climb to 3,000 feet (914 m) and were separated when they ran into heavy fog a few hundred miles from the Azores. The *NC-1* and *NC-3* were forced to land on the water because of the weather. The crew of the *NC-1* was taken aboard a Greek merchant ship and abandoned the *NC-1*, but the *NC-3* was able to drift the last 200 miles (322 km) to the Azores.

Only the *NC-4*, led by Lieutenant Commander Albert Read, continued flying. It arrived in Horta harbor in the Azores after over 15 hours in the air. It was greeted by terrible weather that delayed the trip by another 10 days. At last, on May 27, Read guided the *NC-4* out of the harbor and into the air.

Ten hours after takeoff, the coast of Portugal appeared. The *NC-4* landed at the mouth of the Tagus River just outside Lisbon. It was welcomed by a huge crowd that had been waiting for days. Cannons boomed and bells rang to celebrate the first aerial crossing of the Atlantic Ocean.

After a few days' rest, Read and his crew took off in the *NC-4* for England. They flew along the Portuguese coast and then out over the Bay of Biscay and the English Channel. On May 31, 1919, the *NC-4* arrived at Plymouth, England, where the Pilgrims had set sail for North America 300 years before.

The flight took 23 days and only one of the three seaplanes made it all the way. It was a giant step forward. Even

The NC-4, *upper right, takes off from Lisbon, Portugal.*

though the *NC-4* averaged under 80 mph (129 km/h), it traveled a good deal faster than a ship. For the first time in history, people had crossed an ocean by air.

Alcock and Brown lift their heavily-loaded Vimy off a field in Newfoundland, Canada. The converted World War I bomber carried them all the way to Ireland.

Chapter 4

NON-STOP
ACROSS THE ATLANTIC

Even though the *NC-4* had crossed the Atlantic Ocean, Lord Northcliffe still offered $50,000 for the first airplane to cross it in one continuous flight. Several teams of pilots were camped in New-foundland with their airplanes, waiting for good weather. There, they were as close to Europe as they could get, yet were still in North America.

One of the crews preparing for the flight was a pair of Englishmen, the jaunty, sociable John Alcock and the more withdrawn Arthur Whitten Brown. Alcock and Brown had con-verted a World War I Vickers Vimy bomber into a plane capable of flying long distances.

On June 14, 1919, just two weeks after the *NC-4* arrived in England, Alcock and Brown took off and headed out over the icy water for a non-stop flight. Their airplane was heavily loaded with more than 865 gallons (3,276 l) of gas for its two 360-horsepower (269-kw) Rolls-Royce Eagle Mark VIII engines. The nearest point in Europe was the west coast of Ireland, and it was 1,880 miles (3,025 km) away. Soon, Alcock and Brown flew into a huge fog bank and discovered their only radio was not working. They

John Alcock (top) and Arthur Whitten Brown (bottom)

electric flying suits. It got colder and darker. They kept getting farther and farther from land. The wind blasted them in their open cockpit. Yet Brown was able to use his navigation instrument, and he discovered they were right on course. Then they flew back into the fog.

A strong tail wind added to their speed, so they should have had enough fuel to get them to Ireland with some to spare. But when dawn came on the morning of June 15, they saw their fuel-flow gauge, mounted on a wing strut, was iced over and impossible to read. Without this instrument, they might use too much fuel and run out before getting to dry land.

There was only one way to get the packed ice and snow off the instrument. Brown climbed out of his seat and onto the top of the *fuselage*, or body of the airplane. He hung on to a strut by one hand, and knocked the ice and snow off with the other, even though he was being frozen by the bitter wind.

Brown got the instrument clean so Alcock could read it and adjust the engines to run economically. The gauge froze up several more times, and each time Brown had to climb out and clean it off.

Finally, the Vimy broke free of the clouds and fog and into clear skies. Almost immediately, however, it flew into a violent storm. The airplane was tossed like a rowboat on the ocean. When it was flying at 4,000 feet (1,219 m), the

were alone, with no way to communicate with anyone. After flying for several hours, they climbed above the fog to give navigator Brown a better chance to figure out where they were.

During the climb, their batteries gave out, and they had no power to heat their

After 16 hours and 28 minutes in the air, the Vimy lands, nose down, in a bog in Ireland.

airplane stalled and went into a spin. Down and down it went, locked in clouds and impossible to control. When they were just 60 feet (18 m) above the water, the clouds parted and Alcock was able to see well enough to pull out of the spin.

The Vimy was battered by more storms and more violent winds. Snow built up on the wings, making the airplane harder to control. The only thing to do was fly much lower, where the warmer air could melt the snow. Finally, the coast of Ireland was in sight.

At 8:15 in the morning of June 15, 1919, two very tired men guided their Vimy toward a large field, but at the last moment, they realized the field was not as solid as they thought. It was a wet, soggy, peat bog. The Vimy touched down, its wheels dug into the soft surface, and it tipped up on its nose. It was not a very classy way to land. But the men were safe, even though the Vimy was badly damaged.

Alcock and Brown were instant heroes. They were given parades, prizes, and knighthoods. After all, they were the first to fly non-stop—1,880 miles (3,025 km) in 16 hours and 28 minutes —from North America to Europe.

John Macready (left) and Oakley Kelly stand in front of the Fokker T-2.

Chapter 5

NON-STOP ACROSS THE UNITED STATES

All the long-distance flights in the first decades of aviation were made by adventurers and explorers. There was no thought of having paying passengers take up space needed for gasoline. These flights were also dangerous. For every successful flight, several others failed and people lost their lives.

There was never a shortage of brave pilots who were ready to fly farther than anyone had flown before. However, airplanes were only slowly becoming technologically advanced enough to fly long distances. For a non-stop trip across the United States, there was the

added problem of flying over the Rocky Mountains with peaks over 14,000 feet (4,265 m). Even in the 1920s, airplanes had trouble climbing above 10,000 feet (3,048 m), which would be necessary for a transcontinental flight.

The U.S. Army wanted to fly non-stop from coast to coast, farther than anyone had ever flown an airplane. No long-range airplanes were being built in the United States, so the Army bought a Dutch Fokker T-2, which was a large monoplane with a squared-off fuselage and a tiny tail. The T-2 was built as an airliner that could carry a few people on fairly short trips. But since the Army wanted the T-2 to carry two people on a very long trip, two big fuel tanks were added to increase its total fuel capacity from 130 gallons (492 l) to 725 gallons (2,746 l).

The cockpit only had space for one pilot, but one pilot could not fly the big airplane for as long as a cross-country trip would take. So a small door was cut into the panel behind the pilot's seat. A second set of controls was put in the passenger cabin where the other pilot would ride. When the first pilot needed to rest, he would climb out of his seat and back through the door into the cabin while the other pilot flew. Then they would switch places and the other pilot would climb into the cockpit to fly the plane.

The pilots, John Macready and Oakley Kelly, had difficult jobs. Each in his turn sat out in the open, with only a small windshield to keep some of the wind blast off his face. The 400-horse-power (298-kw) Liberty V-12 engine was only a few inches from the pilot's right elbow. It was hot, very noisy, and splattered the pilot with oil.

The flight started from San Diego, California. Theoretically, the T-2 would be helped by the winds that usually blow from west to east. Only 50 miles (80 km) after takeoff, Macready and Kelly ran into dense fog in a mountain pass and had to turn back.

The second attempt was more successful. Macready and Kelly flew as far

as Indianapolis, Indiana, where the engine broke down.

For the third attempt, Macready and Kelly started from the East Coast. It would be much easier for the T-2 to climb over the Rocky Mountains after it had burned up 3,000 pounds (1,362 kilograms) of gasoline.

John Macready and Oakley Kelly took off from Long Island on May 2, 1923, and headed west. They climbed slowly;

The long, slim Fokker T-2 drones on its steady way across the farmlands of the Midwest. It flew for 27 hours on a trip that, since the 1950s, has taken about four hours.

the T-2 was heavily loaded with fuel. Soon, one of their instruments began to act up. But Kelly was able to take it apart and fix it in flight.

The pilots changed places five times as they cruised over the Midwest, the Plains, and the Rockies. It was awkward, but it worked. At times they flew through solid clouds and light rain. But the engine ran steadily, and the big T-2 flew right along.

Shortly after noon on May 3, 1923, Macready and Kelly sighted San Diego. They landed smoothly. The first coast-to-coast non-stop flight had taken just less than 27 hours. Suddenly, the United States was not as wide as it used to be.

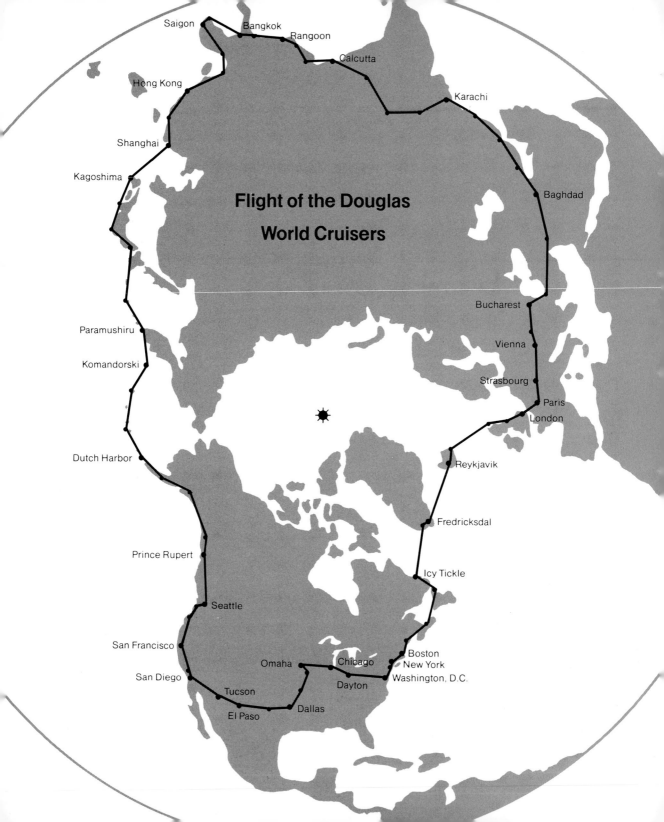

Flight of the Douglas World Cruisers

Saigon
Bangkok
Rangoon
Calcutta
Hong Kong
Karachi
Shanghai
Kagoshima
Baghdad
Paramushiru
Bucharest
Komandorski
Vienna
Strasbourg
Paris
London
Dutch Harbor
Reykjavik
Fredricksdal
Prince Rupert
Icy Tickle
Seattle
San Francisco
Boston
Omaha
Chicago
New York
San Diego
Dayton
Washington, D.C.
Tucson
El Paso
Dallas

Chapter 6

AROUND THE WORLD

The first trip around the world took almost four years. In the early 1500s, Ferdinand Magellan's four ships set out to sail around the world. Because of terrible weather and many mechanical problems, only two ships made it. Four hundred years later, the first airplanes to fly around the world had a very similar experience.

By the early 1920s, the U.S. Army's Air Service wanted to show people what it was capable of accomplishing. After a careful search, the Army found bombers that the Douglas Aircraft Company was building for the U.S. Navy. Powered by dependable Liberty V-12 engines, these airplanes could be flown with either wheels or floats as landing gear.

Four of these bombers were modified and called the Douglas World Cruisers. They were named for cities in four areas of the United States: *Seattle*, *New Orleans*, *Boston*, and *Chicago*. On March 17, 1924, after waiting for the fog to clear, they left Los Angeles, California, and headed north. Their first stop was Seattle, Washington, where they were stuck for two days by bad weather. When they finally took off, the *Seattle*, piloted by flight commander Major

Frederick Martin, was damaged and had to turn back.

After waiting a day for repairs, the World Cruisers flew to Prince Rupert, British Columbia, Canada, 650 miles (1,046 km) away. They arrived in a snow storm and could not take off again until April 10. From there, they flew north toward Alaska, making more stops for repairs. The going was slow and difficult, for the weather was cold and stormy. The World Cruisers struggled along at 85 mph (137 km/h), their two-member crews shivering in open cockpits.

By late April, the *Boston*, *Chicago*, and *New Orleans* had made it to Dutch Harbor, Alaska, and were waiting to begin the next leg. The *Seattle* had lost its way in fog on the way to Dutch Harbor and crashed into a mountain. Martin and copilot Alva Harvey got out of the airplane unhurt and spent a week tramping through the snow to a trapper's cabin.

The three remaining World Cruisers, under the command of Lieutenant Lowell Smith in the *Chicago*, flew over the northern Pacific Ocean, across the edge of Siberia, and down to Japan. All along the way they ran into more mechanical problems and more bad weather. But they pushed on and made

Six of the world flyers—from left to right, Henry Ogden, Leslie Arnold, Leigh Wade, Lowell Smith, Frederick Martin, and Alva Harvey—pose for a photo on their way to Seattle. Of these, only Arnold and Smith actually completed the flight. The other two finishers—Erik Nelson and John Harding —were delayed in San Diego at the time the photo was taken.

One of the Douglas World Cruisers floats among the sampans, or small houseboats, in Southeast Asia.

it across the China Sea in early June, hopping from port to port until they got to Hanoi, in French Indochina (Vietnam).

Smooth water forms a vacuum underneath a float, which pulls an airplane down. The water in Hanoi harbor was too smooth for the float-equipped World Cruisers to take off. At last, the wind picked up and the water became rough enough for the three airplanes to take off

and continue their journey to Calcutta, India. At each stop, there were spare parts, gasoline, and mechanics waiting. Hundreds of people helped service the great flight, even though only a few of them ever got off the ground.

At Calcutta, the floats were removed from the World Cruisers and wheels were attached in their place. The next part of the trip would be over land. In western India, the three planes ran into

Each two-member crew brought a complete repair kit—the contents shown here— with them on their world flight.

a huge sandstorm over the Sind Desert and had to fly almost at ground level. If they had been any higher, the pilots would not have been able to see where they were going.

When the World Cruisers got out of Asia and into Europe, flying conditions improved. They flew to Vienna, to Strasbourg, and then to Paris, where a huge crowd met them. They had to lock their planes in a hangar to keep the crowd from taking parts of the planes as souvenirs. In England, the floats were put back on for the flight across the Atlantic Ocean. The three planes started out on June 30, 1924, for Iceland.

Minutes after takeoff, they ran into dense fog. *New Orleans* almost crashed, but somehow got to Iceland. *Boston* and *Chicago* turned back. The next day they tried again. *Chicago* made it, but *Boston*

had engine trouble and landed on the rough water. Its crew was rescued but the plane was so badly damaged that it was abandoned.

Only two of the original four airplanes that had begun the trip, four and a half months before, were still flying. *Chicago* and *New Orleans* were stuck in Iceland for almost three weeks by broken parts and bad weather. When they were finally able to leave for Greenland, they ran into more terrible weather: rain, snow, and ice. After a week-long wait, they flew on to Newfoundland and then Nova Scotia. The rest of the trip—to Boston, New York, Washington, and then across the United States to Texas and California—was much easier. Each stop brought out friends of crew members and comfortable beds for the night.

One of the World Cruisers makes a perfect water landing.

The two World Cruisers arrived back in Los Angeles on September 23, 1924, six months and six days after they had taken off. They had flown 28,000 miles (45,052 km) in 371 hours of actual time in the air. They had pushed their way through hundreds of miles of terrible weather. They had flown and repaired their hard-working World Cruisers through a trip no one else had come close to completing. In the future, many other people would fly arould the world with faster airplanes and fewer stops, or without stopping at all. But like Magellan, Lieutenant Smith and the Douglas World Cruisers would be remembered for doing it first.

Charles Lindbergh stands in front of the Spirit of St. Louis *before his solo flight across the Atlantic Ocean.*

Chapter 7

SOLO ACROSS THE ATLANTIC

By the 1920s, the Atlantic Ocean had been crossed many times, but always by teams of airplanes or pilots, and always where the distance, about 1,880 miles (3,052 km), was shortest. Raymond Orteig, a French-American hotel owner, offered a $25,000 prize for the first non-stop flight from New York to Paris, about 3,600 miles (5,760 km) apart. It did not have to be a solo flight. Several teams of flyers were already planning for the flight, but a few pilots, among them the quiet, independent Charles Lindbergh, were planning to make the crossing alone.

Lindbergh started with a Ryan M-2 mailplane, a well-proven airplane that he arranged to buy early in 1927. For two months, the entire staff of the Ryan Company worked with Lindbergh to modify the M-2 for the long flight. Longer wings would lift the heavy load of fuel. The cockpit was moved back, and the huge gasoline tanks were put in front of it to keep Lindbergh from being crushed in a crash landing. The windshield was covered to make it more streamlined. Lindbergh could see out the side windows or use a periscope to look forward.

Lindbergh poses in the cockpit of his plane before his famous flight.

The airplane was named the *Spirit of St. Louis* because it was paid for by a group of businessmen from St. Louis, Missouri.

To continue testing the new airplane, Lindbergh flew it from the Ryan factory in San Diego, California, to New York, stopping only in St. Louis. His time of less than 22 hours was a transcontinental speed record.

He arrived in New York on May 12, only to wait for several days as the weather cleared. Other pilots had also been waiting in New York to try for the Orteig prize. Already, four planes had crashed on tests or on takeoff for the transatlantic flight; two of the crashes were fatal. Another plane and its crew had disappeared on the way from Paris.

Early in the morning of May 20, 1927, the *Spirit of St. Louis* was wheeled out

of its hangar at Roosevelt Field, Long Island. Lingbergh checked the plane and climbed in. Shortly before 8:00 A.M., a large crowd watched him bounce down the grass runway and into the air. The airplane was so over-loaded with fuel that it almost did not clear the telephone lines at the far end of the runway. But it got off and soon was out of sight.

For 33½ hours, Lindbergh and the *Spirit of St. Louis* droned eastward. The Ryan's Whirlwind engine ran smoothly. The winds added to his speed. Because his instruments were so crude, Lindbergh did not know exactly where he was for most of the trip. His first glimpse of land was the coast of Ireland. Soon, he was over England and then France. By then it was dark, and he was on his way to a smooth landing after 10:00 P.M. on May 21, 1927, at Le Bourget

Lindbergh skims the water in the Spirit of St. Louis *after his solo transatlantic flight.*

Airport, north of Paris. He was greeted by a wild crowd of 100,000 people. Lindbergh immediately became a world-famous hero.

His flight of 3,610 miles (5,808 km), all alone, captured the public's imagination. He became the idol of Europe and the United States. Before the flight, only people in aviation, and very few of them, had heard of Charles Lindbergh. But after his transatlantic flight, he was one of the most famous people in the world. He took the *Spirit of St. Louis* on a tour of the United States and was welcomed by millions.

Above: Wiley Post set many long-distance records in his sleek Lockheed Vega Winnie Mae. Left: Floyd Gibbons (right) interviews Wiley Post (center) and his wife, Mae, after Post and Gatty's round-the-world flight in 1931.

Chapter 8

SOLO
AROUND
THE WORLD

After the Douglas World Cruisers' six-month flight around the world in 1924, no one tried it again for several years. In 1929, the *Graf Zeppelin*, a German airship similar to a blimp, circumnavigated the world in a record 21 days. Airship fans were very excited, but airplane pilots were upset that a "gas bag" could do something they had not yet done. However, even though airships can travel for the long distances necessary to fly around the world, they are slow. Airplanes are much faster, and, by the 1930s, were becoming more and more capable of long-distance flights.

In 1931, a one-eyed test pilot named Wiley Post set out to prove that an airplane could outdo an airship. He chose an Australian named Harold Gatty to be his navigator. Together, they prepared a sleek Lockheed Vega airliner they named *Winnie Mae*. To increase the plane's range so they would not have to make as many stops along the way, they took the passenger seats out of the cabin and replaced them with a large fuel tank.

Post and Gatty left New York on June 23, 1931, and arrived in Hanover, Germany, late the next day. They grabbed some food and a quick nap and were on their way. Over eastern Europe they flew, and then across thousands of miles of Siberia. Once, they were delayed a half day while teams of horses dragged the *Winnie Mae* out of deep mud at a landing field.

They crossed the Bering Sea to Alaska, then flew over Canada and finally back to New York. It had taken less than eight days for Post and Gatty to fly all the way around the world—less than half the time of the *Graf Zeppelin*. *Winnie Mae*'s crew was rewarded with distance records and fame.

In 1933, a rivalry developed between Wiley Post and Jimmy Mattern, an airline pilot who had tried to fly around the world in 1932. Both wanted to beat the round-the-world record, and both wanted to do it solo. Mattern, flying another Lockheed Vega, took off from Long Island, on June 5, 1933.

Mattern got to eastern Siberia—two-thirds of the way—well ahead of Post's record. But he ran into terrible weather and had to wait several days for it to clear. By the time the weather had cleared, Mattern was far behind the record time, but he was on the way to making the first solo flight around the world.

Then Mattern's Vega ran out of oil and made a crash landing in the northeastern Siberian tundra. The Vega was wrecked, and Mattern's ankle was broken.

On July 15, 1933, a few days after Mattern's crash, Wiley Post took off from New York. His course was almost the same as the one that he and Gatty had flown two years earlier, and he flew the same *Winnie Mae*. In place of navigator Gatty, he had one of the first Sperry autopilots, which could fly the airplane on a straight course for hours at a time.

Post arrived in Berlin right on schedule. After a brief rest, he was in the air again, detouring to Konigsberg, U.S.S.R., to avoid bad weather. He made unscheduled stops in Moscow and Irkutsk to have the faltering autopilot repaired. Even so, he got to Alaska in five days. He made another unscheduled stop in Flat, Alaska, where he landed hard and bent

Jimmy Mattern holds the instruments from his wrecked plane following his attempt to fly around the world solo.

Wiley Post and Harold Gatty stand in front of Winnie Mae.

his propellor. But a new propellor was flown in from Fairbanks and quickly bolted in place.

Two more days and Wiley Post had flown to Fairbanks, to Edmonton for a quick, 90-minute refueling stop, and across the United States. He arrived back in New York on July 22, 1933, after a trip of 7 days, 18 hours, and 49 minutes. In addition to flying the first solo trip around the world, Wiley Post had also flown the fastest.

Jean Batten waves to the crowd in a small town in Australia after her record-breaking solo flight from England in 1934.

Chapter 9

SOLO FROM ENGLAND TO NEW ZEALAND

In 1919, Ross and Keith Smith won a prize for the first flight from England to Australia. They made it in 28 days. Nine years later, Bert Hinkler was the first to make the flight in 15½ days, in addition to flying it solo. Amy Johnson became the first woman, in 1930, to solo from England to Australia. But soon another woman would break Johnson's record and make the first solo round trip between England and Australia.

In 1929, the well-organized, 19-year-old Jean Batten decided that aviation would be more exciting than music, so she sold her piano to pay for flying lessons. Batten had traveled from her native New Zealand to England to study music. It was a time when pilots were taking off in small planes to little-known parts of the world.

Once Batten had learned to fly, she began to think seriously about making long-distance flights, and surpassing the records of other long-distance flyers. First, she planned a trip from England back to her part of the world—Australia and New Zealand. She chose an 850-pound (386-kg) deHavilland Gypsy Moth with a 60-horsepower (45-kw) engine for her flight.

Batten is congratulated by an official at the end of one of her long-distance flights in her Gypsy Moth.

On April 9, 1933, Batten took off from the grass airfield at Lympne, England, and headed for Australia, 12,000 miles (19,308 km) away. She flew, stopped for gasoline, food, and rest, and flew on. In six days, she had gotten as far as India. But on the seventh day, part of the engine broke, and the airplane was badly damaged in a forced landing. She returned to England to make plans for the same flight the next year.

In 1934, Batten had a newer Gypsy Moth with a 100-horsepower (75-kw) engine. Even with all the knowledge she had gained on her first flight, she did not get as far as she had the year before. She ran out of gasoline after fighting strong headwinds and was forced to land in Rome, damaging her airplane.

She was not discouraged, however. In her repaired Gypsy Moth, on May 8, 1934, Batten left Lympne for the third time.

Things went much better, and she flew along, alone, through clouds and monsoon rains all the way to Darwin, Australia, in 14 days and 22½ hours. Batten had beaten Bert Hinkler's record by one day and Amy Johnson's record by four full days.

In April 1935, Jean Batten flew the same Gypsy Moth—its cruising speed less than 100 mph (161 km/h)—back to England in 17 days and 15 hours. She now had been the fastest to fly in a

During her flight from England to Australia in 1934, Jean Batten, in an elegant dress, stops in Darwin, Australia, and is greeted by some aborigines.

light plane, in both directions, between the most widely separated parts of the British Empire.

Batten bought a new airplane—*Jean* —in which to cross the Atlantic Ocean. *Jean* was a low-wing, four-passenger Percival Gull Six with a cruising speed of over 150 mph (241 km/h). In November 1935, Batten flew solo from Dakar, Senegal, on the west coast of Africa, 2,000 miles (3,218 km) across the South Atlantic to Natal, Brazil, in just 12½ hours. With this flight, she became the first woman to fly solo across the South Atlantic.

In 1936, Batten made the trip from England to Australia in *Jean* in only 5 days and 21 hours to break the latest record by a day. She then flew out across the Tasman Sea to New Zealand, despite attempts to talk her out of the flight. She arrived in New Plymouth, New Zealand, after flying 1,200 miles (1,931 km) over open water, in 8½ hours to set another record for a solo flight.

Jean Batten's final record was set on her return to England in October 1937. Again in the Gull Six, she made the long, lonely flight in 5 days and 18½ hours to break the record by more than 14 hours.

Even though she stopped flying in 1940, Jean Batten had earned a long list of important records. She opened the way, both for women who wanted to fly alone for long distances, and for commercial airline flights from Europe to Australia and New Zealand.

Above: Alex Henshaw is carried on the shoulders of his friends upon his return to England on February 9, 1939. English bobbies are there to keep the crowd away. Left: As his friends let him down, the crowd surrounds Henshaw.

Chapter 10

SOLO
FROM ENGLAND
TO SOUTH AFRICA

In 1920, H.A. Van Ryneveld and C.J.Q. Brand flew from London, England, to Cape Town, South Africa, in 45 days. Eight years later, Lady Mary Bailey became the first woman to fly solo from England to South Africa. On her way, she crossed paths with Lady Sophie Heath, who was the first woman to fly solo from South Africa to Cairo, Egypt. Eleven years later, a man became the fastest person to make the round-trip flight, for at least 50 years.

Even by 1939, much of the African continent was wild. Hundreds of thousands of square miles were jungle or desert that had no roads. Only the largest cities had electric power. Alex Henshaw decided to try a flight over the full length of Africa. His small Percival sport-plane, the *Mew Gull*, was one of the fastest racers in England at the time, even though its engine had only 200 horsepower (149 kw). Henshaw had won the 1938 King's Cup Race at 236 mph (380 km/h) in the *Mew*. But a flight over thousands of miles of African wilderness was nothing at all like a pylon race in England.

Henshaw installed more instruments in the *Mew Gull* to help him navigate over unknown territory. He would have no ordinary aircraft radios because there were so few ground stations along his route to give him radio assistance. In addition, he added extra fuel and oil tanks to make it possible to fly as far as 2,000 miles (3,218 km) at a time. Henshaw planned to stop every 1,100 to 1,400 miles (1,771 to 2,253 km), so he would have plenty of fuel left if he had any trouble finding a landing field. Airfields in Africa, in those days, were small and difficult to locate.

Henshaw took off from Gravesend, an airfield east of London, long before sunrise on February 5, 1939. He quickly vanished into the dark sky, headed for the south of France. Things went smoothly, and he roared out over the Mediterranean Sea, on his way to North Africa. At 10:00 A.M., Henshaw spotted the coast of Algeria through a break in the storm clouds.

Henshaw landed at Oran, Algeria, refueled, and took off again. He flew due south over the Atlas Mountains and then over the Sahara Desert. He could see nothing but sand and a few clumps of trees. There were hardly any people, and almost no place to land an airplane in an emergency. Henshaw was alone without even a sputter of talk over a radio.

He made his second stop at Gao, on the shore of the Niger River. The airport had a short, sandy, rocky runway, and the *Mew Gull* almost crashed, but Henshaw landed safely and refueled the plane. After a brief rest, he was off again, barely making it off the terrible runway. A short time later, Henshaw flew into a terrible thunderstorm that tossed his airplane around like a toy on a string.

The entire trip across Africa was a series of battles with the weather. Either Henshaw could barely see where he was going or it was so hot and humid he could hardly breathe. The greatest test

of his flying skill was navigating at night over country that had no visible landmarks.

At last, 39½ hours after leaving England, Alex Henshaw arrived at the first real airport of his trip: Cape Town, at the southern tip of South Africa. He had flown 6,377 miles (10,261 km) in less than half the time that Jim Mollison had in 1932, in his record-setting flight. Henshaw was exhausted, and his muscles ached from fighting with the controls.

Henshaw could have flown slowly and carefully back to England, except that he also wanted to break the round-trip speed record. He rested a full day and then climbed back into the *Mew*'s cramped cockpit and roared off north. The flight should have been easier, since

Alex Henshaw is ready for takeoff from Cape Town, South Africa, on his return flight. An airport official holds his airplane while he gets the engine running.

he was now familiar with the route. But he became violently ill and had an even tougher fight on his hands.

Henshaw battled to stay awake. He flew off course and then found his way back again. More than once, he was within minutes of giving up when he spotted one of the few landmarks he recognized.

The flight back to England took only a few minutes longer than the flight to South Africa, even though he came close to disaster several times. On February 9, 1939, Henshaw landed at Gravesend

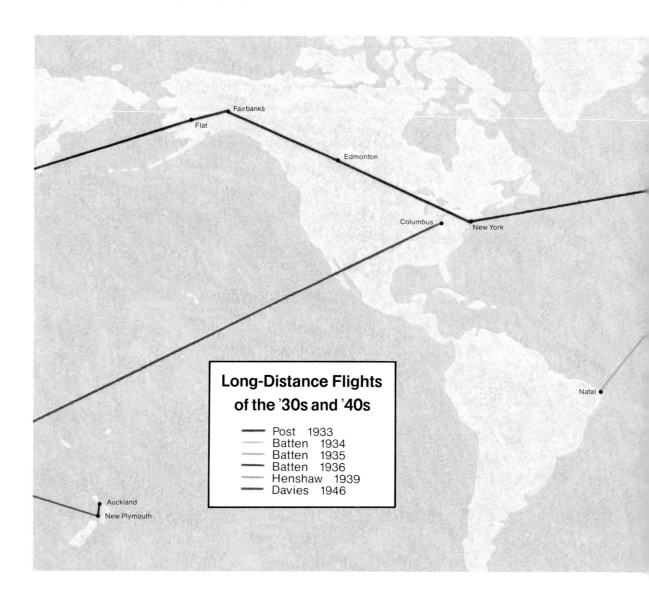

Long-Distance Flights of the '30s and '40s

——	Post 1933
——	Batten 1934
——	Batten 1935
——	Batten 1936
——	Henshaw 1939
——	Davies 1946

airfield, and then collapsed as he was being lifted out of the *Mew Gull*.

It has now been over 50 years since Alex Henshaw flew from England to South Africa and back. His flight still stands as the fastest solo trip ever made between these points.

During the 1930s and 1940s, long-distance pilots flew to many corners of the world.

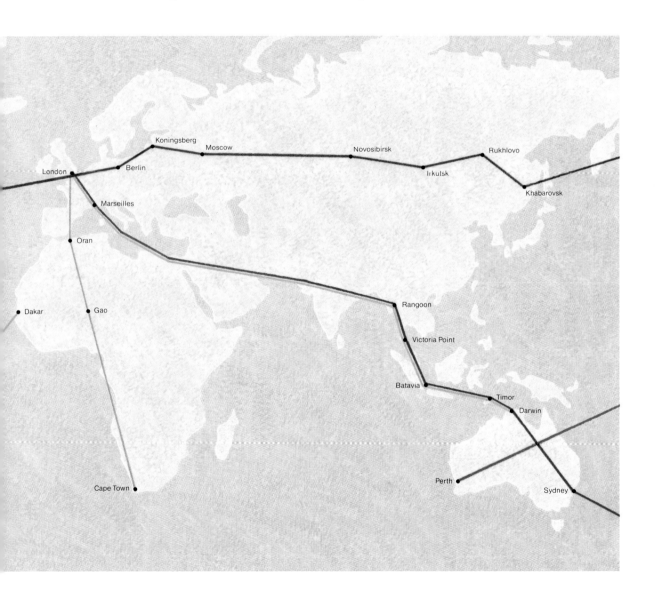

Left: Included in the crew of the Truculent Turtle *are (left to right) Eugene Rankin, Walter Reid, T.D. Davies, and Roy Tabeling. Davies was the aircraft commander on the Turtle's 1946 flight. Below: The overloaded* Turtle *is blasted off the runway in Perth, Australia, by extra small rocket motors.*

Chapter 11

NON-STOP FROM AUSTRALIA TO OHIO

World War II changed aviation as much as it changed most other areas of technology and other parts of our world. Developments in airplanes and engines caused performance to jump ahead faster than ever before. When the war ended, airplanes rapidly continued to improve.

Near the end of the war, Lockheed built the P2V Neptune bomber for the U.S. Navy. It could fly a long way with a heavy load of equipment. As soon as World War II was over, people started thinking about setting records with some of the new, more advanced airplanes. The Neptune was one of the first

airplanes considered for long-distance flying.

One Neptune was modified for an attempt to break the world distance record. All the military equipment, thousands of pounds of guns and armor plating, was taken out of the Neptune. Instead, the fuselage was packed with fuel tanks. An Army B-29 Superfortress had already set the first post-war distance record with a non-stop flight of 7,918 miles (12,740 km), but the Navy was sure it could do much better.

As a joke, the Neptune was named the *Truculent Turtle*. Truculent means fierce, and of course turtles are basically peaceful, quiet, and slow. Since the flight started in Australia, the crew carried a "joey," a baby kangaroo, with them.

The P2V was fueled for the start of its flight in Perth, Australia. Its goal was the West Coast of the United States, 9,000 miles (14,481 km) away. Its two 2,000-horsepower (1,492-kw) Wright engines would consume a lot of gasoline, but if the winds were favorable, it could make it.

Navy Commander T.D. Davies guided the over-loaded Neptune into the air on September 29, 1946, and headed east. On and on over the Pacific Ocean the Neptune flew. The engines ran beautifully, and the winds stayed behind them, pushing them faster and farther. Even before they reached the North American coast, they had broken the world record for non-stop long-distance flying. As they neared the state of Washington, the fuel gauges showed Davies that there was plenty of fuel left. So they kept going—over the Rocky Mountains, then across the Great Plains toward the Midwest. Finally, as the lighter Neptune crossed the Mississippi River, the crew figured out how far the remaining fuel would take them. They landed at the airport in Columbus, Ohio, after the longest non-stop flight in history.

The entire trip covered 11,236 miles (18,079 km). After the Neptune had stopped, Commander T.D. Davies said

that they had used so much gas that "there was not even any smell left in the tanks!" Until the *Voyager* circled the earth 40 years after that flight, Commander Davies and the *Truculent Turtle* held the world distance record for propellor-driven airplanes.

More than 55 hours after they took off from Perth, Australia, the crew of the Navy P2V Truculent Turtle set their plane down at the airport in Columbus, Ohio, to establish a new long-distance record. A crowd forms on the runway to greet the crew of the Truculent Turtle.

For "in-flight refueling," a hose is reeled out from the tail of the KB-29 tanker plane (above). The Boeing B-50 (lower) flies behind the tanker and attaches a long pipe into the end of the hose. Thousands of gallons of gasoline are quickly pumped from the tanker into the Lucky Lady II, as the pilots of each plane carefully maintain their relative positions in the air.

Chapter 12

NON-STOP AROUND THE WORLD

In the 1940s, the U.S. Air Force had been working on a way to transfer fuel from one airplane to another in flight.

The Air Force planned to fly one of its B-50 Superfortress bombers, *Lucky Lady II*, around the world without landing. KB-29 tankers would refuel it in flight.

Lucky Lady II, under the command of Captain James Gallagher, took off from Carswell Air Force Base, near Fort Worth, Texas, on February 26, 1949. When it got over the Azores, *Lucky Lady II* took on thousands of gallons of fuel from a KB-29. As the B-50 flew over the Middle East, it was refueled again. Over the Philippines, and again over Hawaii, it was refueled. The B-50 landed back at its home base in Texas on March 2, 1949, after flying around the world without landing.

The 94-hour flight covered 23,452 miles (37,734 km). The B-50 averaged only 239 mph (385 km/h) because it had to slow down to refuel. Even so, 13 years before John Glenn would be the first to orbit the earth in a spacecraft, Gallagher and his crew circled the earth in an airplane without landing.

Brooke Knapp poses in front of her Gulfstream III, The American Dream, *on a stop in Honolulu, Hawaii.*

Chapter 13

FASTEST AROUND THE WORLD

Many people are afraid to fly. Some overcome their fear, but many do not. Brooke Knapp defeated her fear of flying by learning to be a pilot, and went on to become the fastest pilot to fly around the world.

Knapp enjoyed flying so much that she started a flying business. She became interested in sport flying and started setting records. In early 1983, she flew a Learjet around the world in 50½ hours. Later the same year, in a bigger jet called a Gulfstream III, she set a speed record for flying around the world over the North Pole and South Pole.

In 1984, Knapp set out to fly around the world faster than anyone else. She also wanted to raise money for the United Nations Children's Emergency Fund.

She took off from Washington, D.C., in her new Gulfstream III, *The American Dream*, and flew non-stop to London. From there she flew to Moscow, and then to Novosibirsk, in Siberia. Soon she was off to Beijing, China. She flew to Tokyo, Honolulu, Los Angeles, and back to Washington, D.C. It took her only 45½ hours. Except for astronauts orbiting the earth, Knapp flew around the world faster than anyone else had ever flown.

Prior to their Voyager flight, Dick Rutan and Jeana Yeager climb out of a Long-EZ homebuilt airplane after a long flight.

Chapter 14

NON-STOP
AROUND THE WORLD
WITHOUT REFUELING

In 1986, a non-stop flight around the world without refueling would finally be attempted. In the past, long-distance flights had always been made with standard airplanes, which had been modified with extra fuel tanks, radios, and navigational equipment. But it did not take aeronautical engineers long to realize that an airplane for this particular record would need to be designed for this flight only and be completely original.

Several times, teams had worked for months or years to build an airplane that could circumnavigate the earth without refueling, and then gave up after deciding it was just too difficult. However, two experienced record setters, Dick Rutan and Jeana Yeager, had talked over their idea with Burt Rutan, Dick's brother. Burt Rutan was the recognized genius behind ultra-modern, high-efficiency airplane design in the United States. Soon a very unusual airplane was taking shape on paper.

Voyager was basically designed as a flying fuel tank. At the time of takeoff, the airplane would weigh 2,400 pounds (1,090 kg) and would carry 7,000 pounds (3,178 kg) of gasoline. It needed to be unusually streamlined and unusually

61

light so that the power of its two small engines would be enough to keep it in the air for at least 10 days without landing or refueling in flight.

To make the wings able to lift the fuel, two people, food, and water, they had to have an enormous surface area and still be strong and light. Aluminum and fiberglass simply would not work as they are too heavy in relation to their strength. New composite materials, such as carbon fiber, would have to be used wherever possible.

Many tests were run to make certain that the aircraft was strong enough to withstand high winds and stormy weather. A series of long test flights with partial fuel loads showed that the airplane was solid and the *Voyager* would fly a long way. It was not a pleasant airplane to fly, since it was not meant to fly easily, only far. But the two pilots were experts and they were dedicated to the round-the-world flight.

Early on the morning of December 14, 1986, the *Voyager* and its two-member crew rolled down the 15,000-foot (4,572-m) runway at Edwards Air Force Base in southern California. Never before had the *Voyager* carried its full load of more than 1,000 gallons (3,787 l) of gasoline. It slowly picked up speed as the heavy fuel bent the wings and the tips scraped the runway. At last, after an agonizing

Voyager *flies out over the coast of California on a test flight before its non-stop flight around the world.*

two minutes, the *Voyager* lifted off into the air with only a few hundred feet of runway left.

The winglets on the wingtips were damaged by the scraping and had to be shaken off before they could head out across the Pacific Ocean. The damage only reduced the efficiency of the wings, but it could hurt the crew's chances of completing the long flight.

The problems facing Jeana Yeager and Dick Rutan included weather, navigation, and the lack of space in the tiny cockpit for them to sleep properly or even to stretch. The hours and the miles piled up behind them. On the ground, a radio and weather center was constantly in touch, guiding them around storm clouds and along the path of the most favorable winds.

All the way across the Pacific Ocean they flew, and then across the Indian Ocean. By the time Rutan and Yeager were halfway around the world, they had already broken every important distance record. They had hoped to steer around the southern tip of Africa, but weather problems forced them to cross the continent to keep their tailwinds. Storms over Africa tested the *Voyager* to its limits, but the plane held together and Yeager and Rutan somehow managed to stay alert.

They crossed the Atlantic Ocean, the northern coast of South America, and the thin strip of Central America and were back over the Pacific Ocean again. They turned north and ran into the first headwinds of the trip off the Baja California coast. But they had enough fuel left to make it to where they had started nine days before. Rutan and Yeager circled Edwards Air Force Base and made a smooth landing before a crowd of at least 50,000 people.

In 216 hours, 3 minutes, and 44 seconds Dick Rutan and Jeana Yeager had flown 24,987 miles (40,204 km) at an average speed of 115 mph (185 km/h). They had broken the absolute distance records. They were totally exhausted and impossibly happy to have achieved their goal on the first try.

Yeager and Rutan after their record-breaking flight.

CONCLUSION

From the Wright brothers' first flight in 1903, people have longed to fly farther and faster—to break all the previous aviation records. They have dreamed about crossing the English Channel, the Atlantic Ocean, and even flying around the world.

In the early days of aviation, the pilots making these daring flights were often reckless beginners. Only their luck carried them through. As the greater distances were attempted and airplanes became more technically advanced, pilots became more careful, scientific, and skillful flyers.

Louis Bleriot, Cal Rodgers, Charles Lindbergh, Brooke Knapp, and other pioneers of long-distance flights set the pace for the jet-age society we now live in. Baseball teams fly from New York to Los Angeles in just a few hours. Businesspeople fly from Minneapolis to Tokyo in less than a day. In fact, every time we board an airplane, we are unknowingly relying on the record-breaking, death-defying efforts of the Macreadys and Kellys, the Wiley Posts, and the Jean Battens who made long-distance air travel a reality.

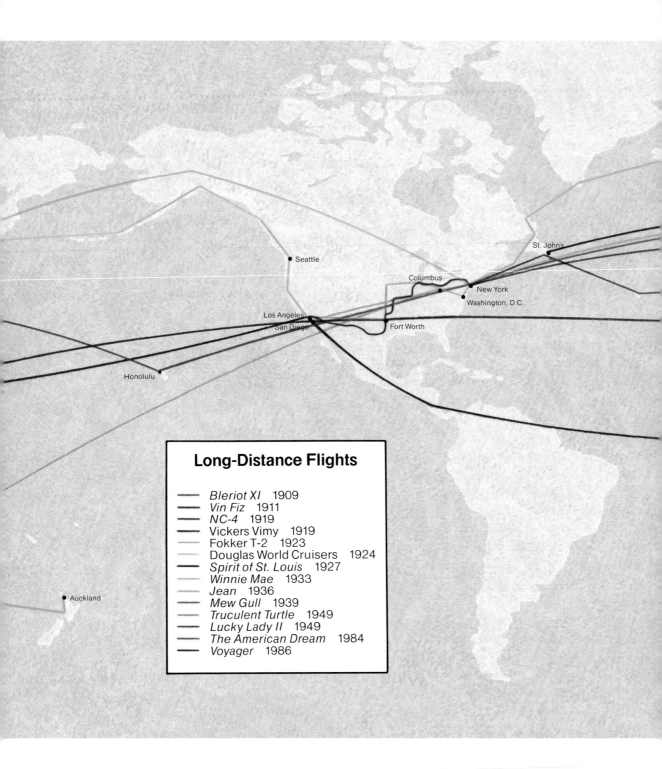

Seattle

Columbus

St. Johns

New York

Washington, D.C.

Los Angeles
San Diego

Fort Worth

Honolulu

Auckland

Long-Distance Flights

Bleriot XI   1909
Vin Fiz   1911
NC-4   1919
Vickers Vimy   1919
Fokker T-2   1923
Douglas World Cruisers   1924
Spirit of St. Louis   1927
Winnie Mae   1933
Jean   1936
Mew Gull   1939
Truculent Turtle   1949
Lucky Lady II   1949
The American Dream   1984
Voyager   1986

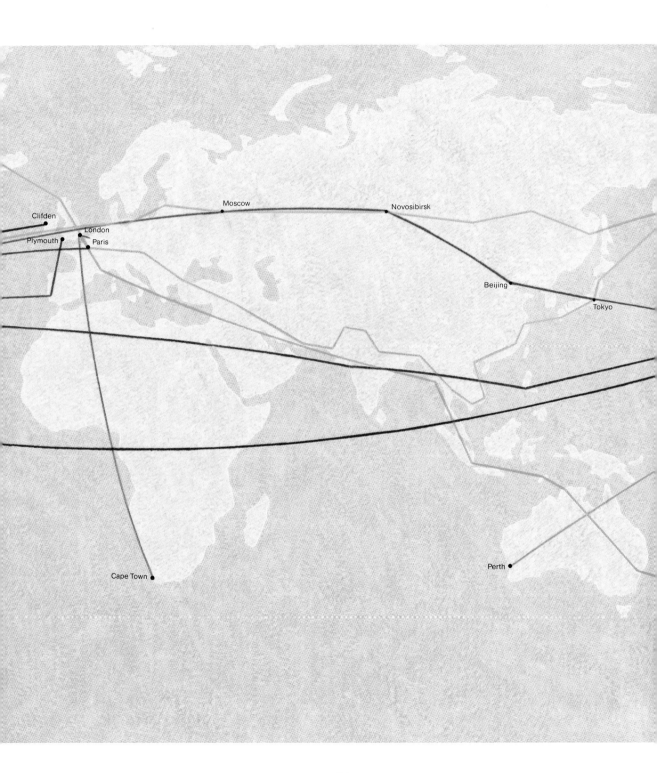

Clifden

Moscow

Novosibirsk

London

Plymouth

Paris

Beijing

Tokyo

Perth

Cape Town

FOR FURTHER READING

Berger, Gilda. *Aviation*. New York: Franklin Watts, 1983.

Berliner, Don. *Research Airplanes*. Minneapolis: Lerner Publications, 1988.

Davidson, Jesse. *Famous Firsts in Aviation*. New York: G.P. Putnam's Sons, 1974.

Dwiggins, Don. *Famous Flyers and the Ships They Flew*. New York: Grosset and Dunlap, 1969.

Lauber, Patricia. *Lost Star: The Story of Amelia Earhart*. New York: Scholastic Inc., 1988.

Provensen, Alice and Martin. *The Glorious Flight: Across the Channel with Louis Bleriot*. New York: Viking Press, 1983.

Rosenblum, Richard. *Wings: The Early Years of Aviation*. New York: Four Winds Press, 1980.

The Smithsonian Book of Flight for Young People. New York: Macmillan, 1988.

Williams, Brian. *Aircraft*. New York: Warwick Press, 1981.

INDEX

ACKNOWLEDGMENTS: The photographs in this book are reproduced through the courtesy of: pp. 1, 31, 32, 33, U.S. Air Force; pp. 2, 10, The Bettman Archive; pp. 6, 72, Don Berliner; pp. 8, 12, 15, 24, 30, 44, 68, Smithsonian Institution; pp. 11, 14, 28, 50-51, 66-67, J. Michael Roy; pp. 16, 18, 19, U.S. Navy; pp. 20, 26-27, 37, 38 (top), 52 (bottom), 56, National Air & Space Museum, Smithsonian Institution; pp. 22, 23, Mansell Collection; pp. 34, 36, Minneapolis Public Library, Minneapolis Collection; p. 38 (bottom), National Archives; p. 40, American Heritage Center, University of Wyoming; pp. 41, 52 (top), 54-55, Lockheed; pp. 42, 45, UPI/Bettmann Newsphotos; pp. 46, 48-49, Alex Henshaw; p. 58, 71, Brooke Knapp; p. 60, Downie & Associates; pp. 62-63, 64, Mark Greenberg.

Cover photos courtesy of Mark Greenberg (front) and the National Air & Space Museum (back).